Time Steals Softer

Also by George Genovese and published by Ginninderra Press
The Essential Space of Play
Love Letters to the World

George Genovese

Time Steals Softer

Time Steals Softer
ISBN 978 1 74027 408 1
Copyright © text George Genovese 2007
Copyright cover image © 2007 Ginninderra Press & its licensors.
All rights reserved.

First published 2007
Reprinted 2017

Ginninderra Press
PO Box 3461 Port Adelaide 5015
www.ginninderrapress.com.au

Contents

Dream Car	7
A Poet's Office	8
In My Garden	10
Beyond	11
Celebration Day	12
To His Absent Love	13
The Handshake	14
Two Lives	15
Time Steals Softer…	16
To His Sleeping Love	17
The Meeting	18
Birdsong	20
Words and Page	21
Remiss	23
A Black Armband View of History	24
Plato's Cave	27
Perfect Night	28
The Future	30
Into the Night, a Personal Injunction	31
The Architects	32
Dirge	33
2004	34
Reverie in an Office	40
Reverie	41
Fables	42
The Dream	49
Spite	50
In the Collective	51
After the Feast	52
A Poetic Joke	53

An Old Man	55
The Caress	59
The Undiscovered	60
The Sort	61
Cyclops II	63
modern poem	64
The Birth	65
Tree	66
Clock-web	67
In the Ocean of Your Arms	68
Infatuation	69
Confession of a Fable Teller	70
Looking for the Oracle of Rust	72
Monument	73
Empire of Self	74
Prophecy	75
A Sudden End	76
How Many?	77
Hymn to Satan	78

Dream Car

I'm everything a woman should
Be, slinky, smooth and beautiful.
With all my curves just yearning for
The firm caress of shampooed shammies,
I'm dripping wet for the hand that strokes
Me. Loyal to the end, I'll never
Question his authority, but stand
By coyly, there to do his bidding.

When I breakdown from stress
Or sheer exhaustion, I'm not one
To feel abused, and anyway
He loves applying masterful fingers
To my body, so I never make a fuss.

From hood to boot he relishes fondling
My naked parts. You see, unlike
Those other types I never weigh
His mind with commitments or worries,
I have no need to know his heart.

Whether he's hunching over, lying
Under, or snuggly saddled in
My fur-lined lap, I let him take
Control and make him feel like he's
A man. In just five months he's had
Six women, soon this sixth is going
To be scrapped, but me he's had for ten
Good years and there's another twenty
Down the track. My secret's simple,
Most times I just keep quiet, and when
I'm not, I'm purring in his hands.

A Poet's Office

Hollowed eggshells
like eyeless sockets,
the can of dog food
scraped of marrow,
cold fridge-hum in
the neon kitchen,
the clock face peering
through a shadow.

The dust shroud wrinkling
on a table,
damp shavings in
the colander;
dry soup stains
crusted on a ladle
and hanging, sallow,
last year's calendar.

The white tiles chipped
like broken teeth
smile tinted yellow
with nicotine,
their groutless gaps,
grimed with decay,
reek winter's age
of mouldy mellow.

And shopping bags,
like prostrate ghosts
lie crumpled on
the weary table,
displaying logos
like the aureoles
by which a saint's
election's shown.

Dreams hobbling through
the peeling paint,
the cracks and grime,
eddy around
each silent object,
clinging jars
of pepper-corns,
of dill and thyme,

or run from darkened
corners like spiders
pouncing their prize,
each presence clung
by portents dark
and undefined,
the unwashed plates
and broken cup – a sign.

In My Garden

Just the fly
and I
and the wind,

the clumps of
dog hair,
dust and butts,

the pear tree,
laden as
ripe rain clouds.

Just suburban
sounds –
the hum of

distant cars
and barks,
the voices

floating through
backyards –
circuitous

dialogues
between
God and me.

Beyond

Much like a fly,
my thinking spins
in spastic circles.

My voice the buzz
that beats the pane
with desperate thuds.

The world within
my grasp, I hit
the invisible limit.

Celebration Day

You see, the fanfare and the hum
about each great achievement
will drown today and time to come
your unaddressed bereavement.

Behind the frolic and the fun,
and tireless jubilation,
the tears, though hidden, yet must run
on which men build a nation.

Throughout each noisy fable, spun
with self-congratulation,
the ghost of sound – indifference dumb,
abets extermination.

To His Absent Love

Whenever I touched you
with the mortal fraction
of this small palm,
maybe I touched
an immeasurable time.

Whenever your blue eyes
seemed pregnant with
unearthly light,
maybe I saw two fragments
of another sky.

Whenever your voice
appeared to call
from somewhere distant,
maybe it fell
from a secret height.

And when the space
you wrapped around
your naked self
was suddenly vacant,
but still lay ruffled

in your silent wake,
discarded like
a morning gown –
then maybe I found you
the very first time.

The Handshake

(In Memoriam Ignacio Mármol, artist and friend)

I still recall that handshake, first of many.
Your grip was certain, firm and dauntless. Any
unfolding circumstance could never unnerve
its confidence and unflinching self-belief.
An artist's hand, no doubt, which only served
a total vision, even to its grief;
for it demanded sacrifice for beauty
above all else, imposing as a duty
on all who braced the power of its grip
to aid it in the work it would make known.
No, I could not foresee how strength would slip
and so much promise quickly overthrown
when first my youthful hand took yours in clasp,
nor feel the cask I'd shoulder in its grasp.

Two Lives

Awake in the dark and lying together,
they harked to the ominous howl of the weather…
She nestled, secure, on the curve of his shoulder
and pillowed in comfort dwelt on the years ended,
and how, even now, just *his* arms could hold her
through ripe days of love perpetually splendid.
Outside the wind hissed, the rain it kept pouring,
the petulant trees were lashing the windows
like furious strangers they both were ignoring
entreating a shelter from where the wind blows.

Awake in the dark and lying together,
they harked to the ominous howl of the weather…
She felt his chest heaving, trembling beneath her,
and scented the mouth whose kisses she savoured,
and thought on the years like one drunk on ether,
how faithful she'd been and never once wavered,
how faultless her heart had weathered each storm
and shone like the sun through darkness and doubt;
and while contemplating joys to be born
he struggled to tell her that he wanted out.

Time Steals Softer…

Time steals softer than the clouds,
floats a suppler course than moisture
spreading through their bowels; rarer
than invisible vapour spinning
to a shroud, time darkens heaven's
eye and creases summer's brow.

Time falls softer than the dust,
passes by ungathered, never
heaping to a crust. Sequestered
and unyielding in a silent
smudge, it creeps behind the grime of
corners and the reek of rust.

Time steals softer than a thief,
robs the robber's hand that tightens
on its secret knife. With sudden
leaps it grips the hands concealed in
gloves and stealth, and overcoming
them, reclaims their deeds itself.

To His Sleeping Love

In the dim room my love lies sleeping;
her brow and cheekbones stand like pale
white plateaux in a sea of darkness…
Her mortal face, a fragile trace
of failing light – where two suns burned
an absence gathers inside two chasms.

The Meeting

How old you suddenly
appear in sunlight.
Your rippled face betrays
the stolen years.

The lustre of your hair
equivocates
between its native blonde
and foreign grey.

With bodies tending in
opposed directions,
our eyes escaping past
mechanical words,

we skirt around the one
remaining vestige
that seized our steps –
the memory of

a mutual friend. Not long
before, entrusting
my over-ripe regards
to her through you,

I heard no word return;
despite your smiles
I knew this was no lapse,
but friendship's end.

Blank years had intervened
and left no shred
of love, not even the
pretence of chagrin.

I feign what little care
I can and wish
you well. You smile as you
anticipate

my fond regards to her
whose word you wish
you could return, but I
withhold her name.

Of all that's altered through
divided years,
your prudent smile is all
that hasn't changed.

Birdsong

A birdsong –
we make no difference between
the bird and what it sings…

A birdsong –
we never doubt the world
that's floating in its throat…

A bird sings and men talk –
but men distinguish between
their words and things,
their world lies hidden
behind their talk…

A birdsong –
none doubt the bird
who sings his being…

A birdsong…

Words and Page

(Three Variations on Grey and White)

I

Perhaps
a white
winter sky

and here
and there

a smudge
of grey.

II

A field of snow
with lines of grey
t
r
a
v
e
r
s
i
n
g
it; impressions of
a man who passed
and left these shallows
where shadows gather.

As if more than snow
in nothing more
than snow dissolving,

his tracks before you.

III

Across a space,
out of surrounding fog,
grey traces of bare trees,

of knotted outlines
nascent through
the mist, of hibernating

lamps and rooftops
sheathed in cocoons
of winter silk –

the vision of
a world emerging
from its sleep.

Remiss

That rusty nail
I often passed
along the road

protruding like
a vicious tooth,
that many passed

with self-preserving
circumspection
but none removed,

and all who crossed
avoided like
a spider's fang

or serpent's mouth…
Who could have known
that rusty tooth

would bear the bitter
venom that took
a loved one's life?

A Black Armband View of History

I

The Amnesiac

Disarming, the amnesiac,
who makes the known world strange;
who moves uneasily among
us here, as if the yielding ground
might drag him into an abyss;
whose ghostly eyes, two echoes of
a self that's lost its light, betray
a terror self-annihilation forgets.
He plagues us, this amnesiac;
with every puzzled act or glance
dismembered from itself, he calls
us liars, says we never shared
a common time and place, and, since
he knows no past, it's common sense,
no alien other can lay claim
to the buried burden of yesterday.
There keeps a killer in those eyes,
a slayer in that shameless face
we hardly recognise as ours –
(mother, father, sister, son.)
And such remains our kindred horror,
such the seduction we must fight –
he'd make us abettors to this lie.

II
Australia

Let us tell you of the dead –
we sing…

But you have lost the ears
and so you say – 'the wind'.

It is the dead who truly know –
who speak,
and when you pass a sacred place
unmindful of respect,
it's us abiding in a branch
who trip your feet.

And let us tell you of the living –
they don't inhabit the land,
but, bounded by their dreams,
remain in regions of sleep;

uncomprehending that they walk
on blood and bone (the dead will moan
in every print the living leave)
they dream the past is said and done
and set in monuments of stone.

'Forget us not!' the dead cry out,
'Forget us not! We are the past
you carry in your blood – to cast
us out of memory would be
a crime you set against your time,
losing the chance to grow with us
in sorrow.

Grief so wrongly parted
leaves us both no rest, and you
who will not compass loss as arm
to arm will never know compassion
past your moment of strength...

Oblivious of our singing, we,
the dead, lament for you, the living...

Forgetful of us, you will be
the slaughterers of yourselves.'

Plato's Cave

Amid a play of phantoms to a grave
I'm left with but a question in their flight –
Are we the bondsmen chained in Plato's cave?

Does substance ebb through every sensory wave
Escaping past an unseen source of light
Amid a play of phantoms to a grave?

Despite the men who boast no doubt, and rave
Of their dominion in this fruiting night,
Are we the bondsmen chained in Plato's cave?

What lordly brow, what conqueror's hand can stave
Off time, delay a dream or frail delight
Amid a play of phantoms to a grave?

Behold! what lies there broken that was brave,
And hear an error mock what once was right –
Are we the bondsmen chained in Plato's cave?

Beyond a new world waits, but a bound slave
Affirms his depths remain the only height.
Amid a play of phantoms to a grave
Are we the bondsmen chained in Plato's cave?

Perfect Night

Give me a creaking door
that opens on a silver night,
a dog's bark snouting warm
the summer air,
a rickety chair
by the battered table
I lean on as I stare
at a long-dead star;

and on this table let there be
the constellations of
my days and nights:
an old chipped ash-tray
and a glass of beer,
the incidental bits and pieces
of daily traffic collected there;

and thereabout a moth or two
that arc my head,
whose circling echo dreams
that ring around my mind.

Let there be voices of calm
amid the brimful stillness:
the singing of crickets,
a whispering breeze,
a benevolent ease
that rises like a psalm
with the rustle of each leaf.

Then laden with that ease,
as full and generous
as heaven is with stars,
so let there be a bed
and in that bed
a lover lost to sleep
to whose recumbent form
I bear a bouquet of dreams
in my embracing arms.

The Future

(On seeing his lover walk out the door)

You sudden seemed a walking corpse
beyond your days of careless grace,
and as you passed with smiling lips,
I saw a skull supplant your face.

And when you calmly stroked your hair,
and pulled your coat about you, tight,
it seemed you drew a horrid shroud
to warm you through eternal night.

But you knew nothing of the dark
that spread like fingers, poised to clasp,
nor felt the sorrow grip my heart
as you approach(ed) oblivion's grasp.

Your steps soon ebbed along the hall
and left me centred on the flow
of vanished sight and sound, to dread
this prelude of what must be so.

Into the Night, a Personal Injunction

Do not forget the wide-eyed waking in
the night – staring into nothing.
This terror, known before,
yet always soon forgotten –
each time as if for the first time,
this death you wear like a second skin.

Not the mere knowledge of mortality,
an abstraction surveyed from afar,
but the intimate intruder
knocking at your eardrums
as you, before yourself, your being
most truly yours, admit this stranger.

Inessentials fall; your greater share of life
is pure illusion. Only this is real –
the darkness and a feeble throb.

Never to turn away from this abyss,
never to lie to yourself again,
never to squander an instant of light –

to keep the fidelity of death for a guide.

The Architects

In such a room as this decisions were made,
a little grander perhaps, with polished floors
and fine lace curtains stirring in the breeze.
Around a table just like this, adorned
with bright, fresh flowers sweetening the air,
men like us met, exchanged their pleasantries
and calmly set about their work. There, with
the clarity of architects absorbed
in their designs, their voices only challenged
by warbling birds outside, they patiently toiled
until their vision began to take shape.
Gnawing the ends of pens, or absently
tapping erasers over blueprints filled
with faceless stats, they coolly ironed out
their plans and schedules with meticulous care.
Through labyrinths of turgid calculations,
interminable revisions and negations,
they settled on an economical means
of cleansing and recycling human waste.
And when, through tedious hours of diligence
confronting technical problems, and resolving
the details for the necessary deadlines,
they duly finalised a workable plan,
whole populations fell with the slash of
a pen. On ordinary chairs like these,
creaking as they leaned back to contemplate
their work, they felt the weary satisfaction
of those who know the magnitude of their
endeavours would be great. Then they had tea.

Dirge

This world where we stand,
this world we breathe
is all we've ever known;

and yet as her kin,
I know not why,
we mete her out such scorn.

Why this contempt,
this hateful abuse,
why treat her like a whore?

The child who would wrong
his mother thus
were better off unborn.

To say, 'But ignorance,'
seems far from home,
men learn where there's a call;

but we only learn
to butcher more
and gloat when knives are drawn.

O mother of mothers,
blood of our blood,
I hear you weep and moan,

but from your travail
I ask, 'What life,
when death's the seed we've sown?'

2004

(For Scott Thurling)

It was a year of knocks and bruises
when I was short of breath
and shorter still on money.
My house creaked loosely all
about me, as did my mind
and body, rotting, rusty,
barely withstanding the
onslaught of the wind.

A year of accident
and death, of one step forward,
three steps back, near breakdown,
and nervous attack, of stops
and starts and pregnant pauses,
stillborn causes, shocks,
and good intent gone slack.
A calendar of weight

and worry where just the bills
kept faith, the wider world
as sick and sorry as
my broken back. It was
a year of guts, no glory,
and parasites who bled
me dry while they grew fat.
A ball and chain of a time,

tax and tithe, surcharge
and levy, oh God, a solar
grind so dismal-dark
and heavy I'd rather soon
forget! It was a time
I guess like any other,
a gurgling funnel
formed of empty fret.

But in that year I felt
myself especially sick.
I drowned in alcohol
and fuelled myself on
nicotine. I laid a path
as black as tar or Guinness
about my heart and mind,
and through a haze of smoke

and beer, shot forth full steam
past dreams of earthly
paradise to see where I
might end. Fallow, sallow,
barely a shadow on
my snail-slow-slime unwinding
track, I fell through every
cunt-wide chink and grimy

crack of this foul world, the while
despairing I should ever
rise again. For in that year
I mourned the human face,
that wanton globe of horror
I still dread, a woven nest
of thorns and shame where I,
a babe and feeble egg,

lay at the mercy of
the ravenous predator,
bird of prey, my yellow
yolk tinged red, a dying
ember, dripping down
an evil beak as I
cried out that day! Oh cruellest
face, inhuman, a knob

or tuber risen from
the clay, what were your eyes
are gloaming slits, your mouth
a sphere of shining darkness,
your ears the spirals centred
on their silence and nostrils
breathing out decay;
the seven gates are shuttered

and with ascendant nonsense
seal their god of death…
Oh in that year men creaked
like cracked automatons,
machines of rag and oil
without a driver at their
cogs, their wheels slow grinding
in a futile slog, their piston

hearts congealing with
the gathered dust of empty
thought – oh chug-a-chug-chug,
a-chortle and chug and choke
to death with barely the semblance
of a bestial snort…Yes in
that year I fell with men
and lost belief in any

hopeful dream and even
shunned the memory
of an animal soul.
With barren equivocation
that crooked year's truth
zigzagged between
a sad banality
and revelation of

a black futility,
the dour eye's scope and margin,
each broken horizon
and hard-earned vision caught
between a cage of coded
bars. A numb and knowing
time of numbers, where soul
was sullied beneath desire,
and the cold and physic eye

shook off its superstition,
met memory of soul
with ironic smiles
and barely hidden derision.
A time where thought oozed through
a dying manikin,
depositing wisdom in
a pool of scum.

Oh husk and dust and dusk!
Oh slaughtered child amid
the mad and raucous merriment,
I let go the sacred soul
and watched it buried,
perhaps beyond return,
to find that man no master
of his own salvation,

not when he scorns what once
proved most his own,
nor kingdom come and God
alone, but something not
yet risen, something not
yet human, something not
divine, something in
between imagination

and reality's form;
still in a state of creation,
words and music seeking
the beauty of a song,
something worthy to
be joined and given in
the marriage that will make
not man, not God, but one!

Oh dream, frail dream,
I fall between this fair
remembrance of a fulsome
plenum and each occluded
hour agape with a red
incision, to wait with accustomed
dread and the weight of worry,
the final cataclysm!

Reverie in an Office

The neon blots all traces of daylight –
he envies those who have the window seats.
The sound of stacking files, the PC's hum –
he ticks the boxes on his A4 sheets.
He rubs his tired eyes, and turning right,
catches a cornered glimpse of sky and sun…
The eucalypts, lulled gently by the breeze
and tinged with mellow light, seem joyous when
they sparkle; when, from out their rustling hearts,
the wattle birds go spearing insects, then
with sharp and skilful sweeps, remount the trees
with throaty cries. As from a dream he starts,
and where he thought an outward gaze looked up,
sees his reflection in a cold teacup.

Reverie

(The Golden Thread)

The beauty of your repose,
the low hum of your lips…
I fancy that such peace
and its attendant dreams
must be the needlework
of gods. Embroidered like
a mirror to yourself
are all the secret sigils
spun of your golden thread…
Deft hands they have, these gods,
but richer still remains
the fabric of their work.

Fables

Oh, for that 'Once upon a time'

when Jack and Jill could still disport upon that hill
without suspicion of what they did up there,
and 'tumbling down' did not immediately imply
some tragic fall or sexy tryst…
Oh well, poor Jill's a hooker now, I'm told,
and Jack's quite satisfied acting as her pimp.

And then, there's Jack-of-the-bean-stork fame.
If this was Jack, Jill's friend, I can't
be sure… Most likely not for he laments
that he's the victim now, not an exploiter as one
might call the former Jack. Oh well, do you
recall how brave he was, taking on that giant?

Ha! A pure and utter beat-up that! No hero,
he's such a mess, he sees an analyst
three times a week, and not because he's phobic
of giants or ogres that can grind your bones
or boil you down into a ball of fat. No, not that!
It's just the giant's a paedophile these days

and that's what's really screwed up Jack.
Poor Jack, he feels he's nowhere to turn, no one
who really understands, not even his analyst,
for he just says, in case you haven't heard,
'We now know God is dead… God's your
imago Jack,' that's what he says, 'a transposed

symbol for the giant and the love you lack!
The more you hanker for a perfect end, the more
you'll suffer these terrible nervous attacks!'
And Jack agrees, and speaking of a perfect end,
resolves each session to quietly kill himself.
And then, of course, there's Goldilocks.

Those bears weren't altogether unreasonable
in being upset with that little brat. You know,
they never mention it in that story but
she left an awful mess, especially in their beds!
When they pulled those covers back they were
appalled. The blood and aborted fetuses,

some still writhing in their slow death;
the foul and strange insects and vermin
scuttling and teeming in a tangled mass
and feeding on her corruption was more
than most could bear, even bears! No vice too low,
no perversion left uncountenanced,

that angelic looking Goldilocks revelled in it all,
and drowned any semblance of decency
in filth along the way. Nah, they never tell you that,
those chroniclers. She was even a porn star for a time
and with a face and body like hers did quite okay,
at least at first. These days she's off her head

in a ward for the insane; tertiary syphilis they say.
All gone those golden locks, apart from some
spare tufts of hair. And her hideous face,
pockmarked with weeping pustules, her ulcerated
body and wasted breasts inspire just dread
or pity on those who come her way. But nothing so

much as the manner in which she oscillates
between exhibiting herself to all the orderlies
and falling on her knees to beg forgiveness and pray…
And yes, Cinderella's prince had an Oedipus complex.
That foot-fetish of his was all about reclaiming
his mother's absent penis. Cinderella was just

a substitute. Of course we must have romance
and so his unctuous charm and *savoir faire* infallibly
won the day. She spent her days molly-coddling him
and he spent his lasciviously eyeing her feet.
If stifling domesticity and a drab routine devoid
of drama or death can be a tragedy,

then their married life was so. She wanted love,
a moment of passion to annul the tedium of it all
and he just demanded that they try that slipper on,
'Once more, just one last time, once more!'
Inevitably he ended up working for Adidas as CEO.
Call it capricious luck or fateful irony, but of all

those old familiar fellows of that 'once upon a time'
it's just the big bad Wolf who really found his calling.
Made something of himself, that Wolf – went into politics
and, with hindsight, what better choice could he
have made? His native cunning, his deadly eloquence,
his incisive wit when it comes to exploiting

the frailties of trusting natures, and his oily
hypocrisy in tandem with a perfect lack
of scruple was bound to yield success in such a sphere.
Poor Little Bo-peep can call out all she likes to those lost sheep,
they've gone off with the Wolf and they'll not return.
The promise of greener pastures was more than their

unreflecting nature could resist. Full stomachs
and comfort, pleasant and secure surrounds, what more
could they want? Sometimes, maybe, they felt
a little uneasy when they'd see his fiery eye
and toothy grin intently fixed on them,
but that's because he loved them all so much

he'd say. And truly, he did take pains for their welfare.
He loved to see them fill their stomachs
and fatten up. And they were more than happy
to oblige, despite that they could sometimes hear
a distant Bo-peep's entreaties grow frantic as night
approached. And what did it really matter if

occasionally one of their plump companions suddenly
disappeared? Perhaps he'd foolishly wandered
out of the Wolf's most earnest care and got
himself in trouble? Oh well, that was somebody else's problem.
Speaking for themselves, they were more than satisfied
with their good fortune and the Wolf was always able

to sooth their fears. The Pied Piper of Hamelin saw
the Wolf had made a savvy move, saw where
the advantage lay, made up with the city officials
who'd cheated him and returned all the children
his piping had wooed away. Back they came
with mobiles at their ears or bobbing to their iPods,

rapping of bitches, guns, gang warfare and sluts,
all finely tuned to what was in and all
attired in the latest style. Yes back they came,
world-weary and this before the age of ten.
So there they sat, the Piper and the Wolf,
one counting his sheep, the other his money,

when who should come along but the Emperor without
his clothes, a colleague and old friend.
'You're just in time,' they cried, 'we were about
to feast on some roast lamb!' They exchanged
a knowing glance to add, 'And oh, what rare
and beautiful attire adorns your frame!'

The Emperor smiled and said, 'Yes, there's
a bit of a funny story about all that!
You know, at the carnival yesterday when I
paraded naked, got caught out lying to myself
and all my subjects, a child cried out the truth –
'Look,' he said, 'The Emperor is naked!' Well I

was flabbergasted, the cheek of the child
to undermine my authority like that!
To embarrass me and foist the burden of
integrity on me, the Emperor! And that
when all my subjects were content to go along
with my farcical fairy tale! Well, let me tell you,

I had him thrown in chains for sedition, in a dungeon,
and there he'll rot…' 'Hear, hear!' the others said.
'Fortunately,' he went on, these fearful times
compel men to remember what's important to them,
their own skin, and so they held off laughing,
or even questioning, despite the grotesquerie

of the ridiculous sham.' 'It's okay,' the others said,
'put it behind you and have a piece of lamb.'
And there they sat about their fire as night approached,
the Piper, Emperor and Wolf and feasted on their fare,
while in the distance one could hear Bo-peep
forlornly cry, 'Come back, come back lost sheep…'

And in a damp and grotty dungeon one feeble voice
was crying out, alone, 'Oh, for that 'once upon a time,'
when things worked out, and truth would win the day.
If not for me, some hope, I wish it for some other,
for anyone, anywhere, that somewhere in this world
grown old, old and sick before it's time, someone

might have some luck and despite impossible odds,
"live happily ever after".'

The End

The Dream

I dreamed the day of darkness came
when men no longer owned a light
that shines from them and not the sun.
Encompassed by the boundless night,

I saw (when once the sun had died
and shattered stars fell thick as hail,
and darkness, spreading sable hands,
had smothered all with one black veil)

those men all tossed like grains of sand
or torn like scattered tufts of cloud,
and whirling madly in the gloom
fell weak with strong, and meek with proud.

All wind-blown, insubstantial men,
pitched to and fro like frenzied phasms,
till, swallowed by that howling void,
they spiralled down forsaken chasms.

Then, woken to the shriekless dark,
this shook me more than all their cries –
no light beyond the cindered sun's
persisted burning in their eyes.

Spite

Because I've felt the darkness lick my heels
and gnaw the substance of my soul, and found
no other's hand for hope when I have seen
so many others full of hope and joy;
because I've dearly longed to be among
your merriment and reap an equal share
of that sweet laughter as would make me yearn
to yield you back an equal store, yet had
throughout no invitation, but rather, felt
the terror of abandonment and despair,
that I bring forth instead this vicious act!
Like one who wishes to create but finds
his only power's to destroy, my hand
imprints its name to this inferior work.
To you, whom fortune blindly favours as
indifferently as it has hindered me,
who look bewildered and would ask, 'But why?'
I give your happy innocence this reply:
Because, amid my desolation, *you*,
whose heights remained beyond my grasp
but whose descent could equal mine, have made
me twist us into balance – twined as one.
For you who still demand a reason's rhyme
I say – I envied you that happiness
which never might be mine; there is no 'why'
but common suffering, and that's my evil's sum.

In the Collective

Lost in thought,
I stop at the street crossing.
When others move
I automatically cross.

Lost in thought,
when others cease their paces
I stop and wait.

Lost in thought,
I trail a leader who
suddenly breaks his pace –

a mortal moment
a car is coming
our light is red!

We all jump back…

Lost in thought,
I almost took the step
that ended thinking

and left me
wondering about
the movement of nations,

if each step taken is
a careless brick on brick,
a hammer forging a new furnace.

Lost in thought,
are self-absorbing thoughts
building another Belsen?

After the Feast

You made the best attempt but now you know
the path you took's the one you would avoid;
you end precisely where you would not go!

So, sighing with a belly-aching throe,
regretting hunger gulled to being cloyed,
you made the best attempt but now you know

this aching weight is all you have to show
in place of where a gnawing pang annoyed,
you end precisely where you would not go!

Again the grape's allured you with its glow,
again you've drunk for joy, by drink destroyed;
you made the best attempt but now you know

that each high hope precedes a wailing woe
and fulsome lust an empty lie employed,
you end precisely where you would not go!

In each fulfilment, foiled, you sense it's so –
a sensual act belies a spiritual void.
You made the best attempt but now you know,
you end precisely where you would not go!

A Poetic Joke

(*A collection of eye-rhymes for an age that lacks ears*)

When looking for a charming rhyme
that cannot fail to move,
I thought no ardent lover's heart
could doubt the word of love.

And yet you say no rhyme at all
is given to your ear,
far from a smooth and sutured verse
you hear a painful tear.

'Too flat!' you sigh, 'a rhyme mistimed,'
and add, while yet you grieve,
'the music of a chiming heart
went seeping through a sieve!'

And with that splendid head you bow,
you add, 'All beauty's gone!
You've lost a lively sonorous flow
and left a hollow bone.'

To you it would have been more sure
the poet's art to prove,
by figuring love as wholly pure
and rhyming it with dove.

You seem to dream that love is sung
with no uncertain word,
but love is mingled bliss and pain
and music 'mid discord.

For me, love's more a vagabond
who wears a tireless boot,
but even so, for all he strives,
he's *still* prone to a stumbling foot.

And so, dismayed, I turn away,
and parting from you now,
I'll take my leave but leave my love
and hope that it may grow;

And while you doubt my artless song,
I doubt the doubter, though,
for in its heart, all rhymes apart,
love's music surges through.

An Old Man

> We work towards a harvest of memories.

He nodded, muttering to himself,
his gaunt face, hovering in the gloom,
lit by the glow of radiant coals.
'Bonehouse where the spirits dwell,'
he said with firefly eyes ablaze,
and puffed a plume of tumbling smoke.
He bowed his silver head and smiled
aloud, 'I feel the spirits waft aloft
beneath the faded thatch. I hear
them wisp with soft and wistful whispers.'

Desultory reflections of
another's eye rode a doubtful gaze
on curlicues of blue-grey smoke.
'Just the cockroaches breed in there,
the nidus of the spider swells
with fattening eggs; perhaps a mouse
or two might scurry through the hall
or down beneath the rotted floors,'
he said, and paused to drink, and then
went on, 'The electric meter's ceased
to turn a time or measured pulse,
its cobwebbed face, anonymous,
encrusted by a coat of dust
no longer sees the light of day.
There, in the ancient living room
where suns indifferently pass
amid the hushed and gathered shadows
of grimy corners, odd creaks cry,

the crash of mouldy plaster cracks
the long-drawn silence, falls and fades.
In there you'd see that plaster heaped
like fallen ash, the ribbed husk of
that room stripped naked, here and there,
with nothing but the musty dark
debouching from the holes and gaps,
the rising smell of damp and earth.
The artefacts of habitation,
old furniture and broken cups,
the treasured plaything of a child,
a train or doll discarded lie,
newspapers strewn with faded print
and tales no one recalls all heaped
unmissed and heedless in the gloom,
the mirrors stand eternal, faceless…
No, nothing stirs, or if it does,
stirs only by an empty draft.'

'But no,' the old man sighs, his eyes
grown moist. 'I see and hear them all.
There's Florry, Laurie, Jim and John,
and Emma, Barry, Lyn and Jane…
And ah the smell of evening roast
amid the glowing fireside mirth!
The clinking, tinkling cutlery

and glowing warm and glugging wine,
its blessing spread upon the din
of ease and friendly company.

And even now, with purple lips,
they smoke and joke and yarn and talk
of never-ending days, of tasks
performed with toil or satisfaction
and all tomorrow's hopes and wants,
trials and triumphs to be won!
By God that Laurie's a card, quick off
the mark with some risque riposte!
Jeez, his rodent face so makes us laugh!
And can't you hear? Jim strums his old
guitar, Barry strokes the piano,
now listen to the music, sweet,
as all of us in chorus sing.
Oh so attuned, we lightly sing
and sway and smile, the circle of
our faces radiant with the soft
and rising music in our souls!
And here, amid the laughter, in
my arms is Emma, sweetest of all –
my sister-soul and friend and wife.
Of all there is to win of good
and generous humanity's heart,
of luck and love to have, yes she
is best! Now listen, isn't her voice,
so pure in tone and rich in charm,
so true a token of a soul
of simple perfection, lacking nothing,
complete in guileless joy and whole
in beauty unadorned, oh hear
her trilling like a lark, oh hear,

you hear?'
'No, I hear nothing, and
confess do no one see…'
'But I tell you
she is here, in my arms! And by
my God her singing rouses me
to tears of joy!'
'It's late and you
are tired. Weariness plays tricks
upon us all. It's squalling out,
the cruel wind stirs these vagaries
in you; how often it can seem
to sound like singing, or a cry
or mocking laughter.'
'You hear nothing?'
he asks, a crooked tear now spilling
down his cheek.
'Just the vacant wind.'

The Caress

(Thanks, Silke)

She wonders how the surface of her palm,
mere fragment to the flesh on which it runs,
yet somehow yields him wholly to her touch,
as if a drop of water could contain
an ocean in its minute bounds, or vast
new worlds unfold inside a mote of dust.
She wonders and, beyond all sense and doubt,
believes the greater, resting in the part,
delivers him completely to her trust.
This palm, that rounds the summit of his shoulder,
this naked arm that rings around his neck,
yields, moment past each passing moment, more
than surface to the surface of her flesh.
Here, given out of time to her caress,
her hand dissolves in his invisible depths.

The Undiscovered

The man who laboured for
the perfect sound,
the right shape,
the unrepeatable sense…

Eccentric then,
a wastrel,
unapproachable oddity
and laughing stock.

Ennobled now through death
they hail him genius,
significant,
a paradigm of sense,

but only so because,
now timeless,
they press him to their service,
make him what they will.

His life, unfettered
by formulas,
and none of the above –

he was a man who laboured for
the perfect sound,
the right shape,
the unrepeatable sense.

The Sort

The sort whose resonant stilettos announce
her passing like a soldier on parade,
her distant gaze intent on mechanical
precision…

                        No doubt the ruthless type
who'd bayonet you in the heart with those
stilettos while you lay there prostrate, stunned,
and just about to make a flirtatious remark…

Her made-up face as undetectable as any
commando's blocked with camouflage,
she sports a blazer, black, and long black skirt –
tight fitting – with a slit along the side,
so that her bone-white calf protrudes
as through a gaping wound…

No doubt the sort who bodes of death…

Who shoulders fast her leather bag erect
and rifle-like, on guard; whose breasts
recoil like two machine-guns as she
marches on, impassive, among the slain…

      Who goes victorious from
campaign to campaign, the injured begging mercy
in her wake, and commands obedience,
demands respect, though she might never deign
to offer any in return…
          The sort whose sharp
annihilating vision passes through
you as an oversight as you lay there
shell-shocked, aching in defeat…

Yes, the sort you curse beneath your breath
and know that you could love.

Cyclops II

The rambling Cyclops to the deep, dark wed,
stands taut of limb and lifts his fearsome head;
and at the rosy mouths of reechy caves,
he casts a glazed dilating eye and enters;
then, plying through the dark, he roves and raves
with bloated hunger to their slaggy centres.
Oh here at home amid the gurgling springs
and subterranean chambers, Cyclops sings
of all the spoils he's pillaged on this day.
With sinews taxed by booty to be stowed
he thumps and thunders on his greedy way
till with a sigh he dumps his heavy load.
At last, exhausted in the fetid deeps,
he folds a weary eye, and softly sleeps.

modern poem

so this your journey's end,
the dregs of failed religion,

this empty vessel that will
not nourish nor intoxicate;

this whimper in the dark,
this bare admission…

a poem you call it, this husk,
the brave heart clamped with rust;

the final shrunken space for all
that fails and disappoints

disguised by erudition
and fortified by irony…

no manner of adornment:
the diamond metaphor

or pyrite simile
distracts the eye or ear

or quells the memory
of its descent from highest hope

to facile artistry…
or humourless joke.

The Birth

Relieved and happy you may be, at last,
now that your long and hard travail is past.
And mother, you may triumph too in this,
your feeble son survived his near defeat
and though still weak, yet seems to know your kiss,
and falls to peaceful sleep to your heart's beat.
That long expected gasp and cry, the first
of countless more to come, provoked the worst
of nightmares as you waited for their sound…
But now he breathes, grows pinker at your breast,
you know he'll grow in strength each yearly round.
But mother, what if you knew this child at rest,
redeemed by caring men, will one day swell
with hate for them, make war and earth a hell?

Tree

The Being breathing tree
translucent in the afternoon –
its airy bulk, the muted
blue-beyond shines through –
unfurls a multitude
of tongues who cry – 'I am.'

The Being breathing tree
of rustles hushed and rested –
its silhouetted arms
receding in the solid
dark; the last streaks folded
in a fisted glove –

                                    triumphant.

Clock-web

I'm writhing in a web of meaning
and somewhere lurks the spider, Time;
entangled in these shimmering strands
I dream I've somehow made them mine.

Look how they sparkle in the sun
with many a shifting, brilliant hue,
seductive, full in beauty here,
amid the cool and drying dew.

But all around, above, below,
are swathed and wizened flies
and I, like they who've gone before,
await where silence shrouds their cries.

With each attempt at extrication,
each meaning's thread slow wound
enfolds my senses, over-laden,
until at length I'm slowly bound.

Suspended here in fascination
and certain of a swift defeat,
to love this foe, prepared to yield,
remains a lifetime's masterful feat.

I hear it call, I feel it shift,
in every soft and trembling strand.
Am I prepared? An unannounced
black fang descends, strikes me and…

In the Ocean of Your Arms

In the ocean of your arms
I am the timeless mariner
who navigates his ship
to undiscovered seas.
The froth upon your lip,
the spindrift of the breath
that flecks my face, recalls
aromas wafting from
the mystic east and all
the bounty of new worlds.

In the riptide of your thighs
I ply the panting folds
and swells of this hot south.
Upon a boundless arc,
my pitching vessel mounts
your crests and spirals down
these vertiginous voids –
one summit more and I
must break – to meet, becalmed,
the glad explorer's end.

Infatuation

No greater demon obsession than this malady
afflicts a man, his soul up-heaved and scattered mad,
his sense struck dumb to foolishness, his vitals turned
to churning with wild longing and ferocious dread,
desire at once eschewed and yet pursued through each
delicious, bitterer minute! And no stronger woe is man
than when he's standing on a burning height, light-headed,
his sad eyes fixed on a gorge agape below, resisting
its pull when every atom of his soul demands he just
let go, withholding all he yearns when his attainment
affirms the way by which he's shattered! Frivolity,
folly and madness and an unappeasable aching far
beyond all reigning means of sane, quiescent containment,
a self-immolation either way, though he deny
or seek, though he abstain from hope or win a dream.
No greater demon obsession than this malady
so makes a man most man, most wild, most meek – a woman.

Confession of a Fable Teller

What wise words can undo a stubborn ear's
conviction in the sound course it pursues?
What shaft of light shines through the lines that vex
a brow? With an eternity of wise
words at our service, clearly none've helped you –
you, who still tremble at an angry rod,
you who still hunger in the pitiless cold.
The cry of the millennia still falls silent
before an idol tongue, demanding that
its sovereign Will be done. While I – a scribe
or whistler in the dark? – who sow my eyes
in distant heavens, what triumph can my time
boast, but the endless dead and resurrected
Golgotha's crooked roads to paradise?
What substance but the countless piles of skulls
and unclaimed bones, the silent, crumbling smiles
belying the fervour of my froth? The truth
that you, who need no telling, never told
is written in the scars of your soul; who know
that history's a bandaged corpse which props
itself on limbs of dust before it falls
into a voiceless void; while I, who stand
here at the ruddy dregs of another dawn
with this symbolic bread and wine, could just
as well approach you with a husk to ease
your hunger's pang and vinegar for your thirst.

For you, who know that words remain a pale
and paltry semblance of a man's unsinging
heart, and are feebler still when all they breed
are fallow questions; yes, you know, these words
of tenderness weren't given for your solace,
but fostered for a self-absolving conscience.

Looking for the Oracle of Rust

(for Ignacio Mármol)

Emblazoned on splintered stone
and spilt like time's own blood,
an undeciphered hieroglyph,
a secret calligraphy
or seal withholding
an immense unknown,
it is the rust I seek…

Dim tongue amid the tap
and thunder of unconscious feet,
discarded butts and whiffling
papers in the wind,
the leaves like tears
the trees have shed,
it is the rust I seek…

Where yesterday's papers swirl
about a stain, ingrained,
(like sheets of vapour,
or hazy memories
or a futural spectre)
a dirty red scrawl
none heeds tells all –
it is the rust I seek.

Monument

Rigid she stood. Her mute eyes anchored in
An unassailable distance. Moving stiffly,
She felt herself becoming brittle under
Our gaze, felt that her burnished image fogged
Beneath our breath, that any sudden move
Might lead to cracks – a break – a crumbling wake.

Empire of Self

That where there should have been attunement,
a tyrant heart decreed discord,
and acts of kindness should have reigned
but a rain of hail and thunder roared;

that where a hand should have unfurled
but coiled securely in a fist,
and certain of its sovereign hold
still only seized ambition's mist;

that where time lent a fleeting chance
we squandered mercy's commonwealth,
that overthrew the sceptred hand,
that ruled the empire of a self.

Prophecy

'It is the vision of numbers' – Arthur Rimbaud

And when at last this neon logo of a world
(this painted whore to hell's damnation hurled)
holds fast her filthy belly in travail
and mourns the child she belches with a curse;
and when the last of lies falls like a veil
and she, a carcass wasted in her hearse,
lies deaf to all delirious fools who feast
and fete the coming of her son, a beast
whose fiery brow's bar-coded with Cain's brand,
his number and his price sewn in his skull,
his sovereign eyes cast on a wasted land
where fly-blown idols, felled, amount to null,
then men will win the god of their disgrace,
and dumb with terror rue his human face.

A Sudden End

I never see the coming sagging sinew,
the yellowing or broken tooth,
the lustre of your hair turn grey,
the taut skin creased and folding into wrinkles.

I never hear the tremor of your heart,
the grinding creak of brittle bones,
your heavy wheeze and shallow breath,
or secret aches and whisper-weary groans;

never admit the cloaking animal
about your hopeful, hidden centre,
nor smell its passing scent, your death
wrapped tight about you like a second skin.

No, never see the toiling animal
who heaves and snorts his human words
and seems inviolable, harnessed in
the safety of a metaphysical thought –

Until at last you lie there dead,
your inert eyes half-drawn towards me.

How Many?

How many of us learn too late,
ours was the All that could be had?
There is no greater glory than
the world a heart can usher in,
no fuller beauty than we prize
or make, nor than a generous mind
and soul allow to see and be.
No riches more than we conceive,
no stronger joy than we confer,
our tongues sing praise or else profane,
our eyes oppress the world with darkness
or blossom with a radiant beam.

How many sorrow then upon
the crest of their last summit, 'Ah,
I never knew the glory of an hour,
if I could have just one again,
how I would linger on a kiss,
and dally on another's smile,
how I would read all nature's secrets
unfurling in a bud and leaf,
how I would savour just that moment
as if it were a grape whose juice
was garnered from the gracious heart
of the world, so pungent and so sweet!'

How many bless their good too late?
My dread is this: that I am one of them.

Hymn to Satan

We hail you, Satan, saviour of our days!
And worship you who bear all mortal blame.
You great corpse bearer of our lidded eyes
And ally to a human hand, disguised!
We hail you Satan with our broken mouths!
Whose shrouded words disown their forking tongues,
To prick no pang that evil's hour is ours
But lay our shame at your inhuman heart.
We beg you, stay, for we'll not stand the stare
Of horror's eyes or sorrow's outraged heart,
Nor face the parted face that asks us, 'Why?'
We need your crooked tale to light our dark!
O merciful champion of averted eyes!
We pray your alien face may grace our glass,
That we might shun the sign that seals our time,
The murderous mark of Cain upon our brows.

www.ingramcontent.com/pod-product-compliance
Lightning Source LLC
Chambersburg PA
CBHW062150100526
44589CB00014B/1763